J ?

Bre W9-BRB-318

After the last dog died : the
true-life, hair-raising
adventure of Douglas Mawson and
his 1911-1914 Antarctic

AFTER THE LAST
DOG DIED

CAMPBELL COUNTY PUBLIC LIBRARY
P. O. BOX 310
RUSTBURG, VA 24588

AFTER THE LAST DOG DIED

**The True-life, Hair-raising Adventure of Douglas Mawson
and His 1911–1914 Antarctic Expedition**

By Carmen Bredeson

NATIONAL GEOGRAPHIC

WASHINGTON, D.C.

CAMPBELL COUNTY PUBLIC LIBRARY
P. O. BOX 310
RUSTBURG, VA 24588

PUBLISHED BY THE
NATIONAL GEOGRAPHIC SOCIETY

John M. Fahey, Jr., President and Chief Executive Officer
Gilbert M. Grosvenor, Chairman of the Board
Nina D. Hoffman, Executive Vice President, President
of Books and Education Publishing Group
Ericka Markman, Senior Vice President, President of
Children's Books and Education Publishing Group

STAFF FOR THIS BOOK

Nancy Laties Feresten, Vice President, Editor-in-Chief,
Children's Books, Project Editor
Bea Jackson, Art Director, Children's Books
Marty Ittner, Designer
Janet Dustin, Illustrations Coordinator
Marfé Ferguson Delano, Editor
Carl Mehler, Director of Maps
Joseph F. Ochlak, Map Research
Gregory Ugiansky, Map Production
Julia Marshall, Indexer
R. Gary Colbert, Production Director
Lewis R. Bassford, Production Manager
Vincent P. Ryan, Manufacturing Manager

Copyright © 2003 Carmen Bredeson
Published by the National Geographic Society.

All rights reserved. Reproduction of the whole or any
part of the contents without written permission from
the National Geographic Society is strictly prohibited.

Library of Congress Cataloging-in-Publication Data
Bredeson, Carmen.
After the last dog died: the true-life, hair-raising
adventure of Douglas Mawson and his 1912 Antarctic
Expedition / by Carmen Bredeson.
    p. cm.
Summary: Describes the life and career of the Australian
explorer, Sir Douglas Mawson, focusing on his 1912
scientific expedition of Antarctica.
ISBN 0-7922-6140-2 (hardcover)
1. Mawson, Douglas, Sir, 1882-1958—Journeys—
Antarctica—Juvenile literature. 2. Australasian Antarctic
Expedition (1911-1914)—Juvenile literature. 3.
Antarctica—Discovery and exploration—Australian—
Juvenile literature. [1/ Mawson, Douglas, Sir, 1882-
1958. 2. Explorers. 3. Australasian Antarctic Expedition
(1911-1914). 4. Antarctica—Discovery and exploration.]
I. National Geographic Society (U.S.) II. Title.
    G8501911.B74 2003
    919.8'904'092—dc21   2003000756

Printed in the United States of America

The body text of the book is set in Galliard.
The display text is set in Confidential and Typeka.

HALF-TITLE PAGE: A shimmering iceberg was
sighted six days after Mawson's Australasian Antarctic
Expedition set sail for the bottom of the world.

TITLE PAGE: Four explorers from Mawson's
Australasian Antarctic Expedition man-haul a heavy
sledge across Antarctic ice.

OPPOSITE: Formed when moist breath meets frigid
Antarctic air and freezes solid, an ice mask covers the
face of an expedition member. Antarctica is the coldest
place on Earth. Winter temperatures average minus
76 degrees Fahrenheit.

Acknowledgments

The author would like to express her appreciation to
the following people for their help in the preparation
of this book:

Mark Pharaoh, curator of the Mawson Antarctic
Collection, Adelaide, Australia, for his expert advice;
Paquita Boston, granddaughter of Douglas Mawson,
for her suggestions and the foreword to this book;
Jessica McEwin and Alun Thomas for sharing stories
and photographs of their famous ancestor.

Credits

Photographs in this book were provided courtesy
of the Mawson Antarctic Collection, Adelaide, Australia.

Quotes from Douglas Mawson and Paquita Delprat
Mawson (listed below) are taken from the following
sources, which are cited on page 63: *The Home of the
Blizzard*, by Douglas Mawson; *Mawson's Antarctic
Diaries*, edited by Fred Jacka and Eleanor Jacka; *Mawson
of the Antarctic*, by Paquita Delprat Mawson; *Antarctic
Eyewitness*, by Charles Laseron and Frank Hurley.

Page 5: Douglas Mawson, 83; Page 8: Paquita
Mawson, 23; Page 13: Paquita Mawson,145; Page 17:
Jacka, 32; Page 18: Jacka, 34 and 47; Page 20:
Douglas Mawson, viii; Page 23: Paquita Mawson, 47
and 50; Page 27: Douglas Mawson, 32; Page 30:
Douglas Mawson, 117; Page 34: Jacka, 106; Page 35:
Douglas Mawson, 131; Page 36, Douglas Mawson,
131; Page 38: Douglas Mawson, 6; Page 41: Paquita
Mawson, 77; Page 42: Douglas Mawson, 160; Page
45: Jacka, 148 and Douglas Mawson, 185; Page 47:
Jacka, 161; Page 49: Douglas Mawson, 200; Page 51:
Douglas Mawson, 201; Page 52: Jacka, 174; Page 53:
Laseron, 150 and Paquita Mawson, 92; Page 56:
Paquita Mawson, 105.

"...the drift is hurled, screaming through space, at a hundred miles an hour, and the temperature is below zero, Fahrenheit."

Taken a few months before he embarked on his own expedition to Antarctica, this studio portrait shows Douglas Mawson at age 29. When Mawson was a boy, his mother ran a boarding house, where she provided meals for the lodgers. Douglas often went shopping for groceries for her and learned how to buy large quantities of food at wholesale prices—a skill that proved to be very useful to him later.

FOREWORD

I have kept the picture that hung near my bed when I was little. It's a photo of a baby surrounded by snow, snug in his fluffy fur coat. The baby's name is Blizzard, a little puppy born in Antarctica, much loved by all the young men who went south with my grandfather Douglas Mawson.

My grandfather had many exciting times exploring the formation of tropical islands in the South Pacific, the ancient rocks of outback Australia, and the ice, snow, and buried rocks of Antarctica. Later in life, he pushed for the environmental conservation of Antarctica and its surrounding waters and promoted the establishment of an international scientific presence on the continent. The achievement that attracts the most attention, however, is my grandfather's solitary trek back to Commonwealth Bay.

This epic trip is just one small part of a life lived to the full as a geologist, keen gardener, farmer, forester, and family man. It will be retold as long as we have the imagination to wonder if we ourselves would have stayed with a dying friend or marched on without him. Would we have chosen a warm bed and a full stomach, or would we have gotten up and painfully pressed on, nibbling just a little food each day?

As one of Douglas Mawson's seven grandchildren and as an Australian, I am proud of his many accomplishments. But most of all I like to remember that when all alone, he kept on trying no matter what went wrong, and plenty did. And that even when there was no hope, he continued to trust in Providence.

Paquita Boston
PAQUITA BOSTON

Douglas Mawson leaned on the rail of the ship *Aurora*, looking down at the crowd gathered below. Thousands of waving, cheering people stood on the dock in Hobart, Tasmania. They were there to see the Australasian Antarctic Expedition begin its long and dangerous journey. Mawson and his crew of 30 men were headed for an unexplored region of Antarctica, the coldest, windiest continent on Earth. They would not be back for more than a year—if they came back at all.

Mawson had a yearning to explore, even from an early age. Born on a farm in Yorkshire, England, on May 5, 1882, Douglas sailed with his family to Australia in 1884. It was on the clipper ship *Ellora* that the two-year-old staged his first daring escapade. According to family stories, Douglas was napping in a cabin with his mother and older brother when a sudden wave slammed against the ship. The cabin door swung open and hit the bunk where Douglas slept. He awoke instantly, wiggled to the floor, and was out the door in a flash.

The child clambered up the stairs to the main deck. He had watched sailors climbing high into the ship's rigging and decided to give it a try. Up he went, using his small hands and bare feet to hang onto the rope. Higher and higher he climbed. The adventure ended all too soon for the curious child. A sailor down below spotted Douglas, scrambled up the ropes, and carried the squirming boy back down to safety.

Mawson's adventurous streak seems to have persisted into his years at the Fort Street Public School near Sydney, Australia. During graduation ceremonies at the school, the headmaster predicted that "if there be a corner of this planet of ours still unexplored, Douglas Mawson will be the organizer and leader of an expedition to unveil its secrets." Little did the headmaster know how right he was.

Aurora makes its way out of Hobart Harbor on December 2, 1911, and heads south toward Antarctica. Thousands of well-wishers on the dock cheer and wave at Douglas Mawson and the members of his Australasian Antarctic Expedition.

Two-year-old Douglas Mawson (right) poses with his brother, four-year-old William. Douglas was about this age when he climbed up *Ellora*'s rigging.

When Douglas Mawson was just 16, he enrolled at the University of Sydney to study mining engineering. He also took some geology classes with Professor Edgeworth David. Geologists learn about the history of Earth by studying its rocks and minerals. Mawson was so fascinated with earth science, he decided to study geology in graduate school. He earned a bachelor of engineering degree in 1902 and a bachelor of science degree in geology in 1904. Soon afterward he was hired to teach geology at the University of Adelaide, located about 800 miles west of Sydney.

Mawson was a popular teacher. He often took his students on field trips to study the rocks and minerals around Adelaide. He also went on many trips alone, to collect material to use in his lectures. There were few roads into the remote back-country, and water was too scarce to support a horse. Mawson solved the problem by buying a motorbike. He loaded up his tools, a tent, some food and water, and he headed into the dusty countryside. Temperatures in the summer often reached 125 degrees Fahrenheit in the shade. During the winter months, the nights got very cold. The extreme weather did not seem to bother Mawson as he conducted his scientific studies. He was especially interested in studying evidence of ancient glaciers.

Douglas Mawson (left) was a member of Ernest Shackleton's 1908 trip to the Antarctic. Shackleton is shown here helping Mawson with plans for his own Antarctic expedition.

Glaciers are formed when fallen snow is packed down by the weight of more and more snow falling on top. The tremendous weight gradually compresses the snow into ice. Because the glacier ice weighs so much, it begins to slide downward. Along the way it gouges rocks and dirt out of the ground and carries this material along. After the ice melts, the sediments remain where they were deposited. Even though there were no glaciers for Mawson to study near Adelaide, he enjoyed examining the sediments they left behind. Imagine if he could see a real glacier in action!

When Mawson heard that Professor David was going on an expedition to Antarctica with Ernest Shackleton, he wrote to David telling him how much he would like to go along. The years between 1895 and 1922 are known as the heroic age of Antarctic exploration. The frozen continent at the bottom of the world was still mostly a mystery, and many wanted to explore its icy landscape. Shackleton had been to the Antarctic with Robert Falcon Scott's 1901–04 expedition. During that trip, Scott made a failed attempt to reach the South Pole.

Mawson (right) was happiest with a hammer
and chisel in his hands, pounding away on
interesting rocks to collect samples for study.
Here he stands with a companion next to
an ancient metamorphic rock in Australia.

"Douglas was so **well** known in the outback that it was not at all hard to contact **him**. Someone always knew where he was."

PAQUITA DELPRAT MAWSON

After the Scott expedition returned home, Shackleton decided to organize his own trip to Antarctica, and he began giving lectures and raising money. Learning that Shackleton was going to be in Adelaide before leaving for Antarctica, Mawson seized the opportunity to introduce himself. So strong was Mawson's curiosity about the frozen continent that he offered his services for free. Shackleton was impressed with Mawson's enthusiasm and signed him up—with pay—for the 15-month trip.

Shackleton's ship, the *Nimrod*, set sail for Antarctica on January 1, 1908. Mawson was very seasick during the first part of the voyage, especially in the cramped quarters belowdecks. One day he staggered up to the main deck to get some fresh air. There was a lifeboat nearby, so he crawled into it to rest. It is there that First Officer John King Davis found Mawson. Davis brought some pears for Mawson to eat. The food revived Mawson, and Davis's kindness led to the beginning of a lifelong friendship between the two men.

The *Nimrod* arrived at Cape Royds, Antarctica, on February 3, 1908. After all of the supplies were unloaded, the ship returned to New Zealand. It was scheduled to return a year later. The 15 men in the expedition crew got busy building a hut to protect them against the bitter-cold winter that was drawing near. Mawson and five others also took the time to climb to the top of a nearby active volcano, the 12,448-foot-high Mount Erebus. As they peered into the massive crater, steam clouds rose to greet them, along with the sounds of hissing and booming.

By the time the first blizzard roared into camp, the men at Cape Royds were snug and warm in their quarters. Douglas Mawson and Professor David shared a cubicle called the Pawn Shop, because it was piled high with microscopes, cameras, notebooks, instruments, and packing cases.

When summer and warmer weather arrived, Shackleton assigned Professor David to lead an expedition to the south magnetic pole, the

Spewing smoke, Mount Erebus looms above the Shackleton expedition's base camp. The expedition hut and stovepipe can just be made out in the center of this photograph. Mawson was among the crew members who climbed to the peak of the active volcano.

On their trip to the south magnetic pole, David, Mawson, and Mackay faced a daunting landscape similar to this one.

point in the Southern Hemisphere at which all the lines of force of Earth's magnetic field meet. (The position of this pole varies with the movement of the magnetic field.) Shackleton himself would head a push to the geographic South Pole, which is located at the very bottom of the Earth. He was determined to be the first person there.

David asked Mawson and Doctor Alistair Mackay to accompany him. They set out from base camp on October 5, 1908, man-hauling two sledges packed with food, tents, extra clothing, tools, a portable stove, sleeping bags, picks and shovels, and fuel. The sledges were so heavy that the men had to pull one ahead, leave it, and then go back for the other one. Mawson was in charge of navigating the journey and drawing maps of the terrain.

Hauling the sledges over rough waves of icy snow called *sastrugi* and up and down ice cliffs tested the men's strength and stamina. The explorers also kept their eyes peeled for crevasses, deep cracks in the ice that make traveling in Antarctica especially dangerous. Often covered with a cap of snow, crevasses can be hard to spot—and easy to fall into, as Mawson's party found. They each tumbled into a crevasse at least once on the trek but were pulled to safety.

Fierce blizzards slowed the men down and kept them trapped in their tent for days at a time. When their food supplies began to run low in December, they were forced to go on half rations. Mawson wrote in his diary on December 22, "Had a thin hoosh, and having had only one other meal today, went to bed hungry." Hoosh was a kind of stew made of dried beef, fat, water, and crumbled biscuits.

Fifty-year-old Professor David suffered a great deal from the reduced rations and severe weather. "The Professor is dreadfully slow now," wrote

After grueling days on the ice, Mawson and his two companions pitched a tent like this one and crawled into their reindeer-skin sleeping bags to try to get warm.

Mawson on December 31. "He does nothing." David got weaker and weaker until he had to turn over command of the expedition to Mawson, who was much younger and stronger.

In spite of the harsh conditions, Mawson was happy to be traveling over territory that had never been explored. He found interesting rocks and kept detailed magnetic readings. He hoped that his observations would provide new information about Antarctica.

After more than three months on the ice, Mawson, David, and Mackay reached the south magnetic pole on January 16, 1909. They planted a flag, claimed the area for Great Britain, and headed toward the coast. On February 3, 1909, after spending a total of 122 days on the ice, the men arrived at the spot where *Nimrod* was due to pick them up. While they were eating dinner in their tent the next day, they heard two gun-shots boom. They scrambled out of the tent and ran toward the beach. The *Nimrod* was steaming toward them, with John King Davis at the helm. Douglas Mawson was so excited when he saw the ship, he failed to watch where he was going and tumbled into a hidden crevasse. "Just as I was descending to the lower shore," he wrote, "the snow gave way and down I went some 18 ft on to the middle of my back, almost break-ing it on a hard snow ridge in the crevasse." The ship's crew hurried to shore, and Davis had himself lowered on a rope to help his friend back up.

David, Mawson, and Mackay's trek to the south magnetic pole turned out to be the expedition's most noteworthy accomplishment. They pro-vided valuable information about the geology, climate, and magnetic varia-tions of the area they crossed. Shackleton had less success. He and his team had gotten within 97 miles of the geographic South Pole and then had to turn back because of low rations and exhaustion. They had started their trek using ponies to pull the sledges. The animals were not well-suited to the cold climate, and all of them died during the first few weeks. Man-hauling the sledges took more time than had been anticipated, and rations began to run short. Everyone managed to get back to camp safely, though, and the crew sailed for home in March 1909.

Upon reaching the south magnetic pole, Mawson (right) set up the camera and Professor David (center) pulled the string that snapped this picture. Then they and Mackay gave three cheers and returned to their tent to celebrate with a little thin cocoa and a hard biscuit.

When Douglas Mawson arrived back in Adelaide, he was hailed as a hero by the citizens and the university students. Professor David thought Mawson was a hero also, and said of his former student, "In him we had…a man of infinite resources, splendid spirit, marvelous physique and an indifference to frost and cold that was astonishing—all the attributes of a great explorer." Douglas Mawson had had his first taste of Antarctica, and he was eager to return for more.

In December 1909, Mawson traveled to England to visit several famous geologists. He was finishing work on a doctorate in geology and wanted to consult with some experts in the field. While he was there he saw the sights with his friend John King Davis. He also met with polar explorer Robert Falcon Scott, who was planning his second expedition to Antarctica. Ernest Shackleton's failed attempt to reach the geographic South Pole meant the race to get there was still on, and Scott hoped to win.

Scott offered Mawson, who now had a good reputation as an explorer, the chance to be one of the men who would make the push to the Pole. Mawson, however, was more interested in being the first to conduct a scientific exploration of the coast of Antarctica that was south of Australia. He agreed to go on

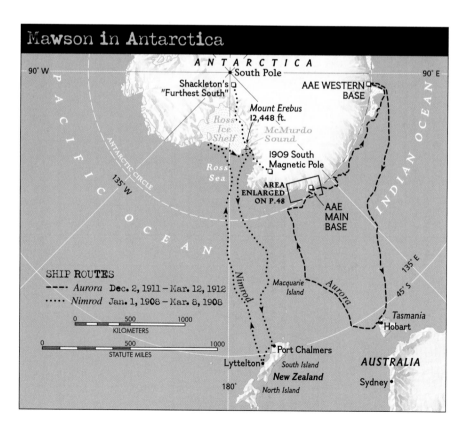

Mawson first voyaged to Antarctica on *Nimrod*, with Sir Ernest Shackleton. His own expedition, sailing on *Aurora*, set up a main base at Cape Denison and a second base 1,500 miles to the west.

When Mawson arrived back in Adelaide, he was met at the train station by a mob of students. They pulled him in a cart back to the university, where he was given a hero's welcome for being one of the first people to reach the south magnetic pole.

the expedition if Scott would allow him to explore this unknown region. Scott considered the matter but then turned down Mawson's request. The expedition's schedule, he said, was already full.

Mawson decided not to go with Scott, but that didn't end his desire to study Antarctica. He began planning his own trip—the first truly scientific expedition to the bottom of the world. During the next year he spent a great deal of time raising money in England and Australia for his Australasian Antarctic Expedition (AAE). A sturdy ship was needed, so Mawson put his friend John King Davis in charge of finding the right vessel. Davis, who would be captain of the ship, located an old wooden-hull whaler called *Aurora* and bought it for the voyage.

While Davis was busy with the ship's overhaul, Mawson appeared before groups such as the Royal Geographic Society to promote the AAE. He explained that little was known about Antarctica and that his expedition intended to study the climate and geology of the frozen continent, along with the local plants and animals.

As word spread, organizations in England and Australia offered money and goods in support of the expedition. Chemical manufacturers Johnson & Sons donated some photographic film that they had tested at very cold temperatures. L.H. Hagen and Company of Norway offered a 10 percent discount on sledges and skis. Other companies donated sleeping bags, tents, clothing, and nearly all of the food needed for the trip. The Australian Association for the Advancement of Science gave a large sum of money. The governments of several countries also pledged their support.

Before leaving England, Mawson hired some key members of his crew. Among them was Frank Wild. Mawson knew Wild from the Shackleton expedition and liked his sturdy, reliable nature. Lt. Belgrave Ninnis and Dr. Xavier Mertz were signed on to be in charge of the Greenland sledge dogs, which were being shipped to England from Denmark. Although Ninnis and Mertz had no prior experience with dogs, something about them must have impressed Mawson.

Mawson returned to Australia in the summer of 1911 to make further arrangements and hire more crew members. The expedition would leave from Tasmania, an island 124 miles south of Australia. Mawson interviewed many who were interested in going on the well-publicized expedition. He was looking for young, healthy men with a spirit

Top to bottom: Dr. Xavier Mertz, Lt. Belgrave Ninnis, John King Davis

"I had seen **him weeks earlier in Adelaide** at some University sports. He had turned and smiled warmly at some friends who spoke to **him**. That grin **did** something to me."

PAQUITA DELPRAT MAWSON

of adventure. He also wanted a crew capable of performing fairly complicated scientific work.

Most of the men Mawson chose were recent university graduates from Australia and New Zealand. Frank Laseron was signed on to collect and preserve animal specimens. Surgeon Leslie Whetter was to be the expedition doctor, and Frank Hurley the official photographer. Full of good humor and adventure, Hurley would do anything to get a picture—even if it involved a great deal of danger. As soon as they were signed on to the crew, the men were put to work gathering supplies.

In spite of his busy schedule, Mawson found time to become engaged to Paquita Delprat, a dark-haired young woman who was nine years his junior. Paquita had some misgivings about the expedition, but she helped Mawson check list after list of supplies and sewed brightly colored bags for storing food. She said, "Although I did not in the least want Douglas to go to the Antarctic, when I realized that he was going whether I liked it or not, he had no keener supporter." They said their good-byes in Adelaide and planned to marry a year later, when Mawson returned from his great adventure.

Ninnis and Mertz load the last of the 39 Greenland sledge dogs onto *Aurora*.

Boxes packed with supplies arrived daily at the dock in Hobart, Tasmania, and were stored in a nearby warehouse. They held sledges from Norway, reindeer-skin sleeping bags, wolf-skin gloves, tents, lumber for the huts, medicine, cameras, scientific equipment, and tons of food. Crates of apples, potatoes, onions, flour, sugar, rice, and dried beans sat beside cases of canned vegetables, fruit, and meat. Members of the AAE crew gathered to sort the mountains of supplies in the warehouse. More than 5,000 individual packages had to be checked and packed into crates. Then the crates were loaded onto *Aurora*. Twenty-three tons of charcoal were shoveled into the ship's hold and drums of kerosene were rolled onto the deck. There was no wood to burn in Antarctica, so fuel had to be taken along. The *Aurora* also needed coal to fire its boiler when the ship was not under sail.

On December 2, 1911, 29-year-old Douglas Mawson and his crew set sail for Antarctica. On the way out of the harbor, *Aurora* stopped at the quarantine station to pick up Ninnis, Mertz, and 39 Greenland sledge dogs. The men had gotten acquainted with the dogs on the 100-day voyage from London to Hobart. Cleaning up after the animals was part of their job, but despite the dirty work, both men got along well with the dogs. Most of the wolflike creatures were friendly, but they had to be tied up several feet apart on the ship's deck to keep them from fighting.

AAE crew members drag supplies ashore on Macquarie Island. Tall, strong, and energetic, Mawson worked right along with the men during the two weeks they spent on the island.

Nine days after leaving Hobart, *Aurora* stopped at Macquarie Island, which is halfway between Australia and Antarctica. The crew unloaded supplies, built a small base, and erected two antennas for radio communication. Douglas Mawson hoped to send wireless telegraph messages from Antarctica to the Macquarie station, which would then transmit them to Australia. If all went according to plan, Mawson's expedition would be the first ever to send telegraph messages from Antarctica. Five members of the AAE team stayed on the island to operate the equipment.

From Macquarie Island, the *Aurora* set out for Antarctica. The men spent hours on deck watching the seas around them come alive. Seals cavorted in the dark blue water and whales blew plumes of spray high into the air.

Aurora steams past an Antarctic ice cliff. Built in 1876, the ship was still in good shape when it sailed with the AAE in 1911. It was made of strong oak planks and had a solid-wood bow covered with steel-plated armor, which was perfect for breaking through ice. Laboratories were added to *Aurora* so marine life could be studied and preserved. Extra bunks were built for the 31 men in the AAE crew, and six freshwater tanks were installed in the hold.

"The ice closed in, and shock after shock made the ship vibrate as she struck the smaller pieces full and fair followed by a crunching and grinding as they scraped past the sides."

AAE crew members construct their base at Cape Denison. The 24-by-24-foot main hut had double bunks around the walls and a large open space in the center for a table. It also had a kitchen, a small cubicle for Mawson's private quarters, and a darkroom for photographer Frank Hurley. The 16-by-16-foot small hut was a workroom containing the telegraph, carpenter's bench, tools, and an area for microscopic studies. The roof of both huts angled down to the ground outside, creating a protected space for supplies and the dogs.

On January 4, 1912, the crew sighted a huge wall of ice to the southeast. Antarctica glistened in the distance. The ship turned toward the 200-foot-tall ice cliff and steamed alongside it for several days. Lookouts kept watch for a place to go ashore. They finally spotted a dark area, and *Aurora* headed for it. The ship steamed into a moon-shaped bay surrounded by a rocky shore on January 8, 1912. The crew lowered a whaleboat into the frigid water, and an advance party climbed on board to go ashore.

Mawson stepped from the boat onto rocks that were teeming with wildlife. It was summer in the Antarctic, and thousands of seals, penguins, and other birds had come ashore to mate and have their young. After a look around, Mawson and his men decided the area was a perfect site for the main base. They called the rocky beach Cape Denison, after a wealthy man who had contributed money to the expedition, and they named the water offshore Commonwealth Bay, after the Commonwealth of Australia.

The men worked fast unloading supplies from the ship. Mawson wanted yet another base established so that more of the coastline could be explored. He put Frank Wild in charge of the next base and gave him instructions to locate it at least 400 miles west of main base. Wild and his team of seven men sailed away on *Aurora* and finally found a good spot for western base on February 13, 1912. By this time they were nearly 1,500 miles from main base. Captain Davis put Wild's party ashore, then turned *Aurora* back toward Australia before winter arrived and trapped the ship in the ice. *Aurora* was due to return in a year to pick up the men at both bases.

Mawson and 17 other men remained at main base. They quickly put up tents and made a temporary shelter out of packing crates and pieces of lumber. Even though it was summer in Antarctica, the temperature stayed below freezing most of the time. The Antarctic summer is short, lasting only from December to February. During these months, the sun never sets. However, it stays low on the horizon and does not produce very much heat. For the other nine months of the year, frigid winter grips the land, and the sun never rises over much of the continent.

The men got busy building the two huts that would be their home during the long winter. Both huts had been prebuilt in Australia and then taken apart piece by piece. Each piece was numbered and shown on a diagram, so the construction went quickly. Everyone slept in the main hut for the first time on January 30, 1912. It snowed hard that night, but the hut was snug. The coal-burning iron stove provided enough heat so the temperature inside stayed at about 45 degrees Fahrenheit. Fortunately the men had plenty of warm clothes to wear. A liquid-fuel generator supplied power for lights. The men took turns standing watch at night to make sure nothing caught on fire. It was a good time for the night watchman to bake bread, wash clothes, and melt ice for drinking water.

There were many blizzards during the month of February. Blowing snow and high winds kept the men inside most of the time. The snow piled up,

"As food for the dogs, there was nothing better than dried seal-steaks with the addition of a little blubber."

One of several puppies born at Cape Denison, Blizzard was the only one to survive. "Needless to say," wrote Mawson, "Blizzard was a great favorite."

almost burying the huts. The blanket of snow acted like insulation, though, and kept the freezing wind from seeping through cracks in the walls.

On clear days the men couldn't wait to get out. They ran and played with the dogs, had toboggan races in the snow, and learned to ski. Xavier Mertz, a Swiss ski champion, was the only one who had experience on skis, so he gave lessons to the others. Belgrave Ninnis and Mertz also harnessed some of the dogs to sledges and took practice runs. The two men had become good friends and were well liked by the rest of the crew for their willingness to help out in any situation.

The men at Cape Denison discovered that their little corner of the world had very high winds. Hurricane-force gales came roaring down the ice cliffs and slammed into Commonwealth Bay. According to expedition records, the average wind speed during April 1912 was 50 miles per hour, and winds of 100 to 200 miles per hour were common during blizzards. They didn't know it at the time, but Mawson's expedition had set up camp at the windiest place in the world.

What did 18 men trapped in a small hut do for weeks on end? Some played cards or read or wrote in their journals. The men also told stories, sang songs, and even wrote and produced a play. A lot of teasing went on, too. Mertz didn't speak English very well at first, and the other men got a kick out of his use of words. And Ninnis, who was called "cherub" because of his young-looking face, never lived down the time he put way too much salt and pepper in the salmon he cooked for one of their meals. The dish looked fine, but when the men tasted it they nearly gagged. Reading chapters of a book aloud after dinner was a popular activity, too, and sometimes Mawson entertained his expedition members with poetry readings.

March brought a special event to the camp. Gadget, one of the sledge dogs, gave birth to two puppies during a terrible storm. One of the pups died, but the other survived and was named Blizzard. The little dog became a favorite of the men and was allowed to spend most of its time in the hut.

The main activity during the long winter months was planning the

Thirty men were depending on Mawson to choose the right supplies for the harsh Antarctic climate. The bags here contain enough food and fuel to last a three-man sledging party about three months.

summer sledge journeys, in which five separate teams would set off in different directions to explore unknown territory. In one part of the hut, a group of men divided food into individual packages for the expeditions. Rations for one man for each day of travel were as follows:

12 ounces hard biscuit 8 ounces pemmican (dried beef mixed with beef fat)
2 ounces butter 2 ounces chocolate
5 ounces dried milk 4 ounces sugar
1 ounce cocoa ¼ ounce tea

When the individual bags were filled, food enough for three men for a week was put into larger bags.

Those who were not dividing food mended clothing or worked on the tents that would be used as shelter on the summer treks. The men knew that poles alone would not hold the tents in place when the fierce winds blew. So they sewed an extra piece of material—a sort of skirt—along the outside base of each tent. Blocks of snow could be piled on top of the skirt

"Noise was a necessary **evil,** and it commenced at **7:30 a.m., with** the **subdued** melodies of the gramophone, mingled with the stirring of the porridge-pot and the clang of plates deposited none too gently on the table."

Expedition members John Hunter, Alfred Hodgeman, and Robert Bage wash up after a meal at main base. Meals were served at 8 a.m., 1 p.m., and 6:30 p.m. The men took turns cooking and were warned by Mawson that their duties were not over until all of the pans and the table had been cleaned. The background image is a list of the expedition's food, showing how it was to be rationed among meals.

"We call it Aladdin's Cave, a truly magical cave for in it perfect peace whilst outside a roaring blizzard....We hang up our clothes by spitting on them and pressing them to the walls."

In Aladdin's Cave, AAE member Robert Bage stirs a pot of hoosh atop an oil-burning stove while expedition photographer Frank Hurley rests in his sleeping bag. Pure ice could be hacked out of the walls for use in cooking. A chart recording wind velocity and direction at Cape Denison forms the backdrop for this image.

to help keep the tent from blowing away. The five poles that formed the frame were sewn into the fabric so the tent could be opened quickly, like an umbrella. The men also made sledge harnesses for themselves and for the dogs. Sledges would be man-hauled on all of the trips except for the longest—Mawson's journey east, which would use sledge dogs.

June 21 brought the middle of winter and bitter cold. The temperature inside the huts barely stayed above freezing. A break in the weather came during August. Mawson, Cecil Madigan, and Belgrave Ninnis took advantage of the calm and set out on a practice sledge journey. After they had traveled just five miles, a blizzard blew in, and the trek came to a halt. The men decided to dig a cave in the ice to use as a shelter and storage place. For two days they hacked out a tunnel and small underground room with their ice axes. They dubbed the place Aladdin's Cave and chipped shelves in the ice to hold an oil-burning stove, fuel, matches, and extra food rations. They spent four nights in the cave before heading back to base.

For months, high winds had prevented the Cape Denison team from getting the telegraph antennas, or masts, up and running. As soon as the masts were raised, they were blown down. In early October, however, they were finally ready. Everyone crowded around Walter Hannam as he sent the first messages to Macquarie Island. They waited anxiously for a reply, but nothing ever came. Then, a few days later, another blizzard wrecked one of the masts and dashed the crew's hope for communication with the outside world. Although the men did not know it at the time, their messages had indeed gotten through to Macquarie Island. The rest of the world knew that Mawson and his men were safe.

In mid-October, hundreds of penguins waddled ashore at Cape Denison, signaling the coming of Antarctica's short summer season. "By October 21 there was a marked thaw inside the Hut," wrote Mawson. "The thick cakes of ice on the roof windows dripped continually, coming away in lumps at lunchtime and falling among the diners...." With the weather getting warmer every day, it was time for the exploratory parties to get going.

"By the middle of October the weather showed but meager signs of improvement, but the penguins came up in great numbers....They climbed up to their old resorts and in a few days commenced to build nests of small pebbles."

An AAE crew member perches among a group
of penguins, who had never seen people before
and were not afraid of them. The men spent hours
watching the entertaining birds. The arrival
of the penguins, which spent the winter in warmer
climes, announced the approach of another
Antarctic summer. Seals and sea lions appeared,
too, along with many other species of birds.

"In no **department** can a **leader spend time**
more profitably than in the selection of the
men who are to accomplish the work."

Mawson, seated to the right of the camera, spends a few quiet moments with his men—and
a curious penguin. The motorboat had been used upon arrival at Cape Denison to ferry men
and supplies from ship to shore.

The five sledging parties, each made up of three men, got ready to head
into unknown territory to explore the terrain and draw maps. The Southern
Party aimed for the south magnetic pole. The Near Eastern Party planned to
explore the coast near Cape Denison. The Coastal Eastern Party would travel
farther east along the coast. The Western Party was headed to the area west
of Cape Denison. The Far Eastern Party, made up of Mawson, Mertz, and
Ninnis, was going to travel to the far east and then go inland for hundreds
of miles. Walter Hannam and two others stayed behind at camp.

One by one, the first four parties set out. Everyone was supposed to
be back at the hut no later than January 15, 1913, when *Aurora* would
return to take them back to Australia. Mawson, Ninnis, and Mertz were

the last to leave. They loaded three sledges, harnessed 16 dogs, and set out on November 10, 1912. It was a beautiful day, and the men were glad to be on their way. The dogs were also eager to run after the long winter. Blizzard, now big and strong, charged ahead with the other dogs.

The good weather did not last long. Storms and rough ice slowed the men down. They often had to help the dogs pull the sledges over sastrugi and up and down ice cliffs. Hidden crevasses also posed a constant danger. One day Blizzard and another dog suddenly disappeared from sight.

Ninnis and a team of dogs set out for Aladdin's Cave to deliver a load of supplies. Greenland sledge dogs are bred to pull and will run until they are exhausted if they are not stopped for a rest.

The last photograph taken of the Far Eastern sledge party shows Mawson, Ninnis, and Mertz, accompanied by 16 dogs, as they set out on their exploratory expedition.

"10 November 1912: The weather is fine this morning though the wind still blows. We shall get away in an hour's time. I have two good companions, Dr. Mertz and Lieut. Ninnis. It is unlikely that any harm will happen to us."

Mawson and his companions found the yelping animals hanging onto the edge of a crevasse by their front paws and rescued them. A few days later, however, Blizzard's luck ran out. When he fell on the ice and broke his leg, the men could think of no way to save their favorite. Sadly, Blizzard had to be shot. Three other dogs were also lost to accidents and illness.

Gradually, as the men and dogs ate through their supplies, the sledge loads got lighter. The men moved everything onto two of the sledges and left the one that was in the worst shape behind. Mawson kept a daily log of their location, temperatures, wind speeds, and conditions on the ice.

December 14 was a clear, bright day. Mertz sang as he led the way on skis, looking for hidden crevasses. Mawson walked beside his sledge about 300 yards behind Mertz. Ninnis brought up the rear, walking next to the second sledge, which carried the most important cargo. At one point Mertz turned and raised a ski pole to indicate he had found evidence of a crevasse. Mawson approached the area with caution and looked for a crack in the snow. He saw the outline, but it seemed like just another crevasse, and the men were accustomed to them by now. He hopped on his sledge, took out his logbook, and started to calculate their position. When he felt his sledge cross an uneven area, he turned and called out to Ninnis to be careful.

A few minutes later Mertz stopped in his tracks and looked back. Mawson turned around too, looking straight back to where Ninnis had been only moments before. But he wasn't there now. Ninnis had disappeared. Mawson jumped off his sledge and ran until he came to the edge of an 11-foot-wide gash in the ice. Two sets of sledge tracks led up to the hole, but only one set continued on the other side.

Mawson yelled to Mertz to bring his sledge and then began calling into the crevasse. "No sound came back," wrote Mawson, "but the moaning of a dog, caught on a shelf just visible one hundred and fifty feet below....Another dog lay motionless by its side." Mertz arrived and the two men got a long rope from the sledge and dangled it into the hole. It was too short to reach the ledge where the dogs lay. Ninnis

A massive rock formation juts out from a glacier that Mawson and his companions crossed on their journey. It was later named Mertz Glacier, in honor of Xavier Mertz.

was certainly even farther down. There was no way to reach him. The men called down to their friend for three hours before giving up.

At 9 p.m., Mawson and Mertz stood by the crevasse and conducted a burial service for 24-year-old Belgrave Ninnis. The rest of the planned journey, as well as the scientific work, was out of the question now. Nearly all of the food had gone down the hole with Ninnis, along with the tent. Mawson and Mertz still had their sleeping bags, a spare tent cover, and the oil-burning stove and fuel. There was only enough man food for one and a half weeks and no food at all for the six remaining dogs. They were 320 miles from base camp. It had taken them five weeks to get this far

A landscape similar to this one challenged Mawson and Mertz as they started back to base camp. The dogs grew weaker and weaker, until finally they were unable to go on.

and would probably take at least that long to return. Still, returning was their only hope of survival. They harnessed the dogs and started for home. "May God Help Us," wrote Mawson.

Mertz and Mawson reached the abandoned sledge the next day and salvaged all they could, including the runners, which they inserted in the spare tent cover to serve as poles. The dogs, who had not eaten for a full day, whined with hunger. The men gave the starving animals old leather gloves to chew. One of the dogs was too weak to go on, so Mawson shot him and fed his meat and bones to the other five dogs. The men took a share for themselves including the liver, which was soft and easy to chew after being boiled. Over the next few days, the rest of the dogs were shot to end their suffering. The men loaded them on the sledge, where they froze immediately and could be cut up later for food.

Soon after the last dog died, on December 28, Mertz grew very weak and layers of skin began peeling off of his body. The men stayed in camp on January 4 and 5, so that Mertz could get some rest. Mawson was eager to go on because every day they did not travel meant less food for the trip back, but he couldn't leave Mertz behind. On the night of January 7, Mertz began raving and having fits. He broke a tent pole while he was thrashing around, so Mawson spent hours holding him down. "About midnight," Mawson recalled, "he [Mertz] appeared to doze off to sleep and with a feeling of relief I slid down into my own bag....After a couple of hours, having felt no movement, I stretched out my arm and found that my comrade was stiff in death."

In the morning, Mawson dragged Mertz's body outside. He cut blocks of snow and covered the body with them. Then he made a simple cross for the grave out of the broken sledge runner and read the burial service. "It was unutterably sad that he should have perished thus," wrote Mawson, "after the splendid work he had accomplished....No one could have done better."

Mawson was now alone on the ice. He spent the next two days getting ready for his solo journey. He boiled the rest of the dog meat, mended his clothing, and cut his sledge in half so it would be easier to pull.

The night before he set out, Mawson's feet felt peculiar. He had not had his socks off for several days, so he decided to take a look. When he peeled the last pair of socks off, the soles of both feet came off in two solid pieces. The skin underneath was raw and bloody. He spread cream all over his feet and tied the soles back on with bandages. Then he put on six pairs of socks to act as cushions.

Mawson set out the next morning. His plight appeared hopeless. It was January 11, 1913, and he knew he could not possibly make it back to main base by the January 15 deadline he had given the other teams. Would Captain Davis and the *Aurora* wait for him?

Treacherous traveling conditions hampered Mawson's pace. Thick snow fell and the ground was crisscrossed with sastrugi and crevasses. On January 17, as Mawson carefully made his was across a crevassed area, the ground beneath his feet suddenly gave way, and the next thing he knew, he was dangling on the end of a rope in a gaping hole.

He thought the end was at hand, but the sledge and rope held. Mawson began hauling himself slowly toward the surface. He had managed to get to the lip of the crevasse when the snow gave way and he fell back into the hole. Should he try again or just cut the rope and end his misery? Mawson wasn't ready to give up, so he began to inch his way up the rope again. When he got to the surface this time, he pulled himself full length onto the snow and wiggled to safety. The effort was so great that he passed out for an hour or two. When he regained consciousness his body was numb with cold. It took him three hours to put up the tent and finally get inside to warm up. Once in his bag, he couldn't sleep. What if he fell again? Would he have the strength to get out the next time?

Then Mawson had an idea. He decided to build a rope ladder and attach one end to himself and the other to the sledge. As long as the sledge did not fall into the crevasse with him, he could climb the rope ladder to safety. This plan proved to be a lifesaver, for Mawson tumbled into several more crevasses and managed to climb out each time.

> "I **had time** to say to **myself** 'So this is the end' expecting **every** moment the sledge to crash on **my head** and **both of us** to go to the bottom unseen below."

Goggles

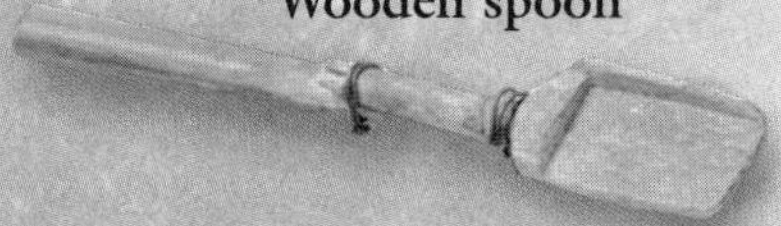

Wooden spoon

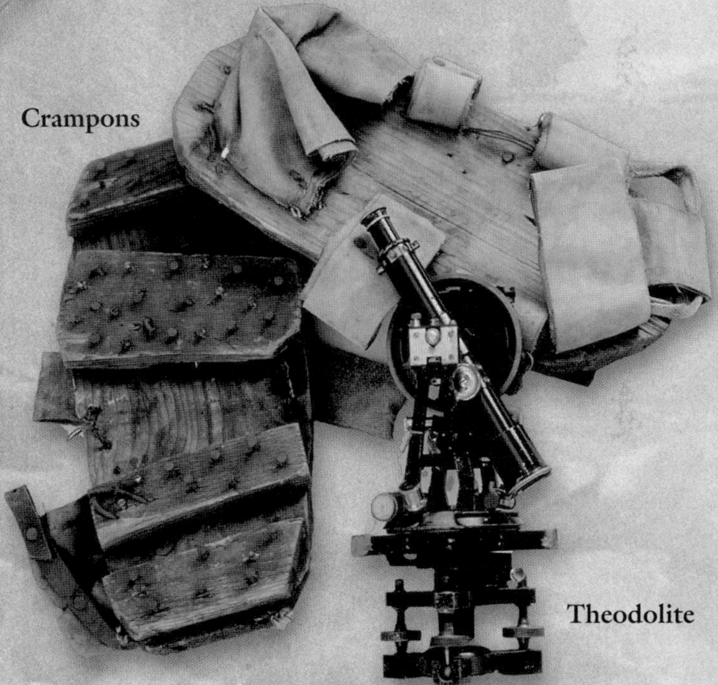

Crampons

Mawson used these items in his desperate trek back to main base. The theodolite, an instrument for measuring angles, helped him navigate. The goggles protected his eyes from snow-white glare and bitter cold. He used spare pieces of wood to make the spoon and crampons. He strapped the crampons, which were studded with nails, to his boots to help him walk across patches of ice. To lighten the weight he had to pull, Mawson sawed his sledge in half with a pocket knife. He loaded only the most necessary items, since he would be hauling the sledge alone.

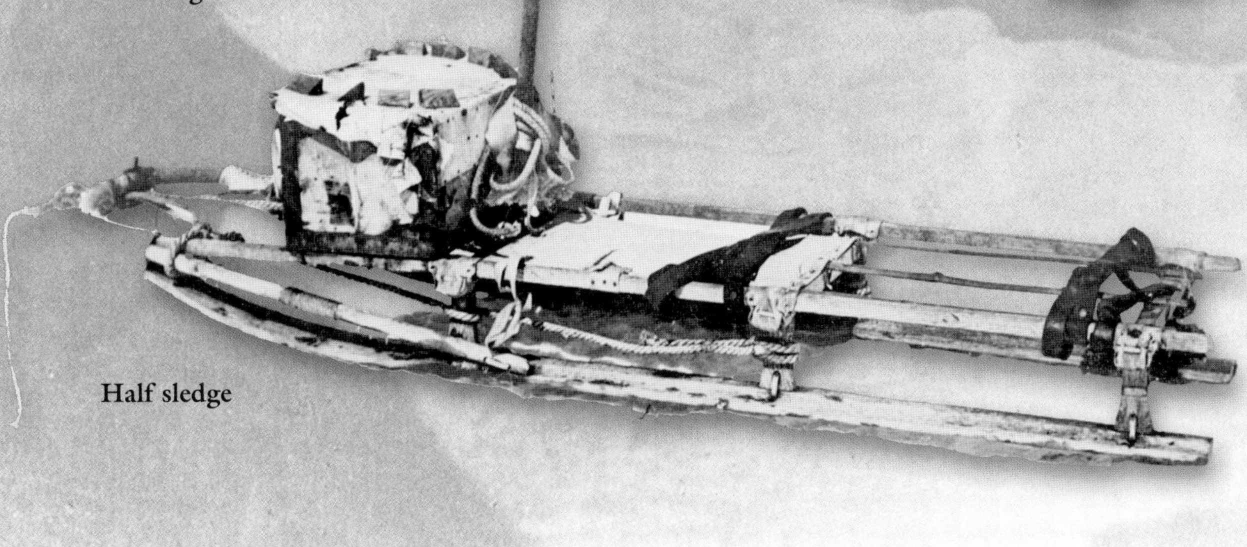

Theodolite

Half sledge

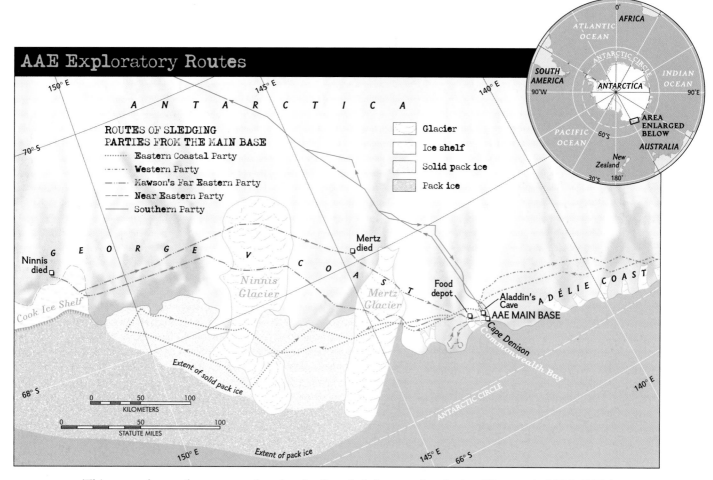

ROUTES OF SLEDGING
PARTIES FROM THE MAIN BASE
.... Eastern Coastal Party
— · — Western Party
— · · — Mawson's Far Eastern Party
– – – Near Eastern Party
——— Southern Party

Glacier
Ice shelf
Solid pack ice
Pack ice

This map shows the routes taken by the five sledging parties during Mawson's 1911–1914 Australasian Antarctic Expedition. Mawson, Mertz, and Ninnis made up the Far Eastern crew.

Mawson made slow progress toward camp. The skin was peeling off his entire body, and his hair and beard were falling out in clumps. His torn feet made each step he took on the hard ice torture. To make matters worse, nearly all of the food was gone. Mawson thought about giving up the fight, but he was determined to get as close to camp as possible. If he died, he wanted someone to find his logbook and diary so Paquita and the rest of the world would know what had happened.

While he was slogging across the ice on January 29, Mawson spotted something dark up ahead. He hurried forward and found a pile of snow covered with black cloth. On top of the cloth was a bag of food and a note from three of his men. They had built the snow cairn just six hours before as they searched for him and his companions. Mawson gobbled some of the food while he read the note. It said that Aladdin's Cave, the refuge that he had helped dig in the ice near main base, was just 21 miles away.

Mawson left at once and managed to travel a dozen miles before setting up camp. The next day he covered only four or five miles. He was so weak that he fell down every few feet and ended up crawling much of the way. On February 1, 1913, Douglas Mawson finally arrived at Aladdin's Cave. He scooped snow from the tunnel's entrance and crawled inside. A beautiful sight greeted him—three fresh oranges and a pineapple! The fruit could only mean that *Aurora* had arrived.

There was other food stored in the cave, and the starving man ate his fill. Then he repacked his bag with rations and crawled to the surface. But when he stuck his head out of the tunnel, a roaring blizzard hit him in the face. The fierce storm drove him back into the cave and kept him trapped for another week. "Think of my feelings," wrote Mawson, "as I sat within the cave, so near yet so far from the Hut, impatient and anxious, ready to spring out and take the trail at a moment's notice."

Back at the hut, the four other exploratory parties had returned safely. Search parties had gone out seeking Mawson's team but had found no trace of the men. Captain Davis kept *Aurora* in Commonwealth Bay, waiting to load up and head west to pick up Frank Wild and his men. If Davis waited too long, the ship could get stuck in the ice.

Captain Davis decided he had to push on. His crew unloaded another year's supplies from *Aurora*. Bage, Madigan, Bickerton, Hodgeman, McLean, and a new telegraph operator, S.N. Jeffreys, agreed to stay at the hut in case the missing men returned. Before setting sail, the ship's crew helped put up the telegraph mast that had blown down the previous October. *Aurora* left for western base the morning of February 8, 1913.

That same morning Douglas Mawson set out on the final five miles of his journey. When he got to the ridge above camp he saw three men working near the hut. As he waved, the men saw him and began running up the hill. They did not recognize their leader at first. He had lost nearly half of his normal 210-pound body weight.

This hilltop view of main base and Commonwealth Bay greeted Mawson when he finally made it back. The tall poles are telegraph masts. The men who had stayed at the base ran up to greet their leader. They listened with tears in their eyes as Mawson told them about the tragic deaths of Ninnis and Mertz.

"Then the rocks around winter quarters began to come into **view**; part of the basin of the Boat Harbour appeared, and lo! there were hum**a**n figures! They almost seemed unreal — was it all a dream?"

Weatherbeaten and weary, Mawson sits for a picture, the first one taken of him after his return to camp. Four days after his return Mawson wrote, "I have shaken to pieces somewhat, and I anticipate it will take some time to pull me up to anything like I was physically before that awful journey home."

The men walked down the hill with Mawson, pulling the sledge for him. They sent a message to *Aurora:* "Mawson arrived. Mertz and Ninnis dead. Return at once and pick up all hands." Captain Davis received the message and turned the ship around immediately. *Aurora* reached Commonwealth Bay, but hurricane-force winds kept it steaming offshore for four days. Davis finally had to leave for western base. He knew that the men at Cape Denison had provisions for a year and could survive. Wild's team, on the other hand, had no extra provisions and might die if left on the ice.

The seven men at Cape Denison faced another long, dark winter. Mawson was too weak to do any work at first. Gradually he grew strong enough to begin taking his turn cooking and standing watch at night. During some of the long hours of watch, Mawson drew plans for a house he wanted to build for Paquita back home in Australia.

The telegraph helped raise everyone's spirits. The men at base camp could finally send messages home and get answers in return. All of the men on Macquarie Island had volunteered to stay another year to keep the telegraph operating.

Paquita Delprat was on Mawson's mind a lot. She had already spent an entire year waiting for him. Would she wait another? He sent a telegraph message to her that said:

```
"DEEPLY REGRET DELAY ONLY JUST MANAGED REACH HUT
EFFECTS NOW GONE BUT LOST MY HAIR
YOU ARE FREE TO CONSIDER YOUR CONTRACT BUT TRUST
YOU WILL NOT ABANDON YOUR SECOND HAND DOUGLAS."
```

Paquita replied:

```
"DEEPLY THANKFUL YOU ARE SAFE
WARMEST WELCOME AWAITING YOUR HUNTERS RETURN
REGARDING CONTRACT SAME AS EVER ONLY MORE SO
THOUGHTS ALWAYS WITH YOU ALL WELL HERE
MONTHS SOON PASS TAKE THINGS EASIER THIS WINTER
SPEAK AS OFTEN AS POSSIBLE."
```

While waiting for *Aurora*'s return, Bickerton and Hodgeman built a memorial for Mertz and Ninnis out of timber from a broken telegraph mast. They carved a plaque and secured it to the base of the cross with large rocks.

On March 16 more good news arrived. *Aurora* had picked up Wild's party, and they were all safely home. The western base crew had explored and mapped a large part of the coastline around their camp. Their year had been a good one, and all eight men were healthy.

The winter passed slowly for Mawson and the men at Cape Denison. They continued to keep track of temperatures and wind speeds. In early October, they began watching for penguins. Day after day passed and no birds came. Then, on October 17, several penguins waddled ashore. A few days later a telegraph message arrived that said *Aurora* was on its way to Cape Denison.

The men cheered as *Aurora* steamed into Commonwealth Bay on December 12, 1913. That night there was a feast in the ship's dining room with

On his way home at last, Mawson (standing, right center) poses aboard *Aurora* with several of his men. Before leaving Antarctica, they had received the sad news of Robert Scott's expedition to the South Pole, which Mawson had been invited to join. Scott and four companions had perished on the journey.

the Macquarie Island crew and Hurley, Hunter, and Correll—three of the original main base crew. They had returned with *Aurora* to pick up Mawson.

The ship stayed in polar waters for another six weeks while the men drew more maps of the Antarctic coastline and collected a variety of marine specimens, including plankton, sponges, algae, and sea stars. Then *Aurora* turned toward home. She arrived in Hobart on February 26, 1914. Paquita

"Douglas and I could not believe we were really married at last and I remember we laughed a great deal."

PAQUITA DELPRAT MAWSON

A month after his return to Australia, Douglas Mawson and Paquita Delprat were married. Captain Davis is in the top left corner of the picture and Professor David is in the top right corner. William Mawson stands just behind his brother's shoulder.

Mawson drew these house plans during his second winter in Antarctica. He and Paquita later built the house and lived in it together for 39 years.

was waiting there for her fiancé, whom she had not seen for more than two years. The couple traveled back home to Adelaide, where Douglas Mawson once again received a hero's welcome.

Paquita Delprat and Douglas Mawson began making wedding plans right away. On March 31, 1914, they were married at Holy Trinity Church in Melbourne, Australia. The day after their wedding they sailed for England, where Mawson planned to write a book about his experiences. He would call it *The Home of the Blizzard*.

When the newlyweds arrived in London, King George V bestowed a knighthood on Douglas Mawson for adding so much to the world's knowledge of Antarctica. The various sledge journeys undertaken on the Australasian Antarctic Expedition had mapped several thousand miles of previously unexplored territory. The AAE had successfully used telegraph communication for the first time in Antarctica. In addition, expedition members had collected and preserved animal, plant, bacteria, and rock specimens. They had also carefully recorded wind, temperature, and magnetic data.

When they returned home to Australia, Douglas and Paquita Mawson built the house Douglas had designed in Antarctica. Their first child, a daughter named Patricia, was born in 1915. Another daughter, Jessica, came along in 1917. Mawson continued to teach geology at the University of Adelaide. He returned twice to Antarctica, in 1929 and 1931, to collect more scientific information about the continent. In 1952 he retired from teaching. That same year, the first Australian research station was established at Horseshoe Bay in Antarctica. It was named Mawson Station.

When he was 76 years old, Douglas Mawson had a slight stroke. A month later he had another stroke and died on October 14, 1958, in the house he had planned when he was in the Antarctic.

A state funeral was held for Sir Douglas Mawson on October 16, 1958, in Brighton. It was attended by many of Australia's leaders and by hundreds of mourners. The church bells tolled 76 times in honor of each year in the life of Australia's greatest polar explorer.

During the short Antarctic summer, seals bask in the sun on floating blocks of pancake ice, which gets its name from its shape.

AFTERWORD

In the introduction to his book, *The Home of the Blizzard,* Douglas Mawson said that Earth is like an enormous jigsaw puzzle, and that each piece of information that is added gives us a more complete understanding of our planet. He was, above all else, a scientist. His curiosity led him to a great unexplored region of the Antarctic.

Scientific exploration was not Mawson's only interest, however. He was also concerned about the wholesale slaughter of whales, seals, and penguins in polar seas. He believed that the continued killing would eventually lead to the extinction of some species. To help protect polar creatures, he pushed to have Macquarie Island declared a wildlife sanctuary, a feat that was accomplished in 1933.

Today more than 40 research stations are in operation in Antarctica. Over 4,000 scientists and support staff occupy these bases during the summer season. Instead of the all-male crews of the past, today's Antarctic scientists are both men and women.

Mawson and his AAE crew were the first to use the telegraph to send messages from Antarctica. Nowadays, information from the frozen continent is at our fingertips. Many bases have websites on the Internet that broadcast current temperatures and wind speeds. Some research facilities, including Mawson Station, also have live webcams that allow Internet users to monitor the activities there. Such technology has given us all an opportunity to fit more pieces of Earth's puzzle together.

Appendix: Vitamin A Poisoning

In 1971, scientists discovered that the livers of Greenland sledge dogs contain huge quantities of Vitamin A. Just four ounces of liver has enough vitamin A to poison a man. Each dog liver weighs about two pounds. Symptoms of severe overdose include peeling skin, hair loss, stomach pain, dysentery, and eventually convulsions and death. Douglas Mawson and Xavier Mertz ate several dog livers during their ordeal on the ice.

The AAE Crew

Main Base

NAME	AGE	ROLE
Dr. Douglas Mawson	30	Commander
Lt. Robert Bage	23	Astronomer
Francis Bickerton	22	Motor engineer
John Close	40	Assistant specimen collector
Percy Correll	19	Mechanic
Walter Hannam	26	Wireless operator/ mechanic
Alfred Hodgeman	26	Mapmaker/ sketch artist
John Hunter	23	Biologist
Frank Hurley	24	Photographer
Charles Laseron	25	Chief medical officer
Cecil Madigan	23	Meteorologist
Archie McLean	26	Chief medical officer
Dr. Xavier Mertz	28	Dog handler
Herbert Murphy	32	Supply officer
Lt. B.E.S. Ninnis	23	Dog handler
Frank Stillwell	23	Geologist
Eric Webb	22	Magnetician
Leslie Whetter	29	Surgeon

Western Base

NAME	AGE	ROLE
Frank Wild	28	Leader
George Dovers	21	Mapmaker
Charles Harrisson	43	Biologist
Archibald Hoadley	24	Geologist
Evan Jones	24	Medical officer
Alec Kennedy	22	Magnetician
Morton Moyes	25	Meteorologist
Andrew Watson	24	Geologist

Macquarie Island

NAME	AGE	ROLE
George Ainsworth	33	Leader/ meteorologist
Leslie Blake	21	Geologist/ mapmaker
Harold Hamilton	26	Biologist
Charles Sandell	25	Wireless operator/ mechanic
Arthur Sawyer	26	Wireless operator

S.Y. AURORA. AUSTRALASIAN ANTARCTIC EXPEDITION, 1911.

A souvenir of the AAE, this picture of *Aurora* features the signatures of the expedition members. Not long after his return to Australia, Mawson sold the ship to Sir Ernest Shackleton, who used it in the Ross Sea during his Imperial Trans-Antarctic Expedition of 1914–1917.

61

CHRONOLOGY

1882, May 5
Douglas Mawson born in Yorkshire, England.

1884
Family moves to Australia.

1898
Mawson graduates from high school at age 16.

1899
Enrolls in the University of Sydney.

1902
Receives bachelor of engineering degree.

1904
Receives bachelor of science degree in geology.

1905
Begins teaching geology at the University of Adelaide.

1908, January 1
Sets sail for Antarctica with Ernest Shackleton's expedition.

1909, January 16
Mawson and party reach the south magnetic pole.

1911, December 2
Mawson's Australasian Antarctic Expedition sets sail from Hobart, Tasmania.

1912, January 8
Establishes main base camp at Cape Denison, Antarctica.

1912, November 10
Douglas Mawson, Lt. B.E.S. Ninnis, and Dr. Xavier Mertz embark on Far Eastern sledge journey.

1912, December 14
Ninnis dies in crevasse.

1913, January 7
Mertz dies.

1913, February 8
Mawson reaches main base.

1913, December 12
Aurora returns to Cape Denison to pick up Mawson and crew.

1914, February 26
Aurora arrives in Hobart, Tasmania.

1914, March 31
Douglas Mawson and Paquita Delprat married.

1914, June 29
Mawson knighted by King George V of England.

1915, April 13
Daughter Patricia born.

1917, October 28
Daughter Jessica born.

1929
Mawson returns to Antarctica on the British, Australian, and New Zealand Antarctic Research Expedition (BANZARE).

1931
Makes second BANZARE voyage to Antarctica. Visits huts at Cape Denison.

1952
Mawson Station established in Antarctica. Mawson retires from teaching.

1958, October 14
Dies at home in Brighton at age 76.

RESOURCES

Books

Ayers, Philip. *Mawson: A Life.* Victoria, Australia: Melbourne University Press, 1999.

Bickel, Lennard. *Mawson's Will.* New York: Stein and Day, 1977.

Boston, Paquita. *Home and Away with Douglas Mawson.* Carnarvon, Australia: Gascoyne Printers, 1998.

Flannery, Nancy Robinson, ed. *This Everlasting Silence.* Victoria, Australia: Melbourne University Press, 2000.

Hall, Lincoln. *Douglas Mawson: The Life of an Explorer.* Sydney, Australia: New Holland Publishers, 2000.

Jacka, Fred, and Eleanor Jacka, eds. *Mawson's Antarctic Diaries.* North Sydney, Australia: Allen & Unwin, 1991.

Laseron, Charles, and Frank Hurley. *Antarctic Eyewitness.* Sydney, Australia: Angus & Robertson, 1999.

Mawson, Douglas. *The Home of the Blizzard.* New York: St. Martin's Press, 1998.

Mawson, Paquita Delprat. *Mawson of the Antarctic.* London: Longmans, Green and Co., 1964.

Rubin, Jeff. *Antarctica.* Victoria, Australia: Lonely Planet Publications, 2000.

Interviews

Boston, Paquita (Douglas Mawson's granddaughter). Interview by the author. E-mail exchanges, 2002–2003.

McEwin, Jessica (Douglas Mawson's daughter). Interview by the author. Telephone, May 2002.

Pharaoh, Mark (Curator of the Mawson Antarctic collection). Interview by the author. E-mail exchanges, 2002–2003; Telephone, February 2003.

Thomas, Alun (Douglas Mawson's grandson). Interview by the author. Telephone, February 2002.

Internet Sources

Douglas Mawson
samuseum.sa.gov.au/mawson/mawindex.htm
Mawson exhibit sponsored by the South Australian Museum and the University of Adelaide.

Sir Douglas Mawson
mawson.sa.gov.au/usesite.htm
Hear the Antarctic wind. Get student research ideas.

Antarctic Connection
antarcticconnection.com/antarctic/weather/index.shtml
Follow weather conditions at the various research bases.

Australian Antarctic Division
antdiv.gov.au/stations/mawson
Read the history of Mawson Station. Watch live pictures from the webcam. Hear a penguin sneeze, a seal yawn, and penguins squabble.

The AAP Mawson's Huts Foundation
mawsons-huts.com.au
See expedition photos and read news of the hut restorations.

South-Pole.com
south-pole.com
Read the history of South Pole explorations.

INDEX

One of the world's largest nonprofit scientific and educational organizations, the National Geographic Society was founded in 1888 "for the increase and diffusion of geographic knowledge." Fulfilling this mission, the Society educates and inspires millions every day through its magazines, books, television programs, videos, maps and atlases, research grants, the National Geographic Bee, teacher workshops, and innovative classroom materials. The Society is supported through membership dues, charitable gifts, and income from the sale of its educational products. This support is vital to National Geographic's mission to increase global understanding and promote conservation of our planet through exploration, research, and education.

For more information, please call 1-800-NGS LINE (647-5463) or write to the following address:

NATIONAL GEOGRAPHIC SOCIETY
1145 17th Street N.W.
Washington, D.C. 20036-4688
U.S.A.

Visit the Society's Web site:
www.nationalgeographic.com